Talking Points and Healing Tools
Helping children after trauma

Jenny R Craig, LCSW, BCD

Insite Strategist, LLC contend clinical recommendations contained herein are the result of extensive author research and review. Any recommendations for individual care must be held up against individual circumstances at hand. To the best of our knowledge any recommendations included by the author or faculty reflect currently accepted practice.

However, these recommendations cannot be considered universal and complete. The author and publisher repudiate any responsibility for unfavorable effects that result from information, recommendations, undetected omissions or errors. Professionals using this publication should research other original sources of authority as well.

DISCLAIMER AND/OR LEGAL NOTICES
The information presented herein represents the view of the author as of the date of publication. Because of the rate with which conditions change, the author reserves the right to alter and update her opinion based on new conditions. While every attempt has been made to verify the information in this report, neither the author nor his affiliates/partners assume any responsibility for errors, inaccuracies or omissions. Any slights of people or organizations are unintentional.
For information on this and other manuals and audio recordings, please visit our website at www.insitestrategist.com or www.gratefulring.com

ISBN-13: 978-0-9832486-4-4
ISBN-10: 0-9832486-4-8

Talking Points Table of Contents

15. Negative Thought Zapper Visualization

16.Creating a Gratitude Ring - Steps to creating an environment where each person's individual strengths are honored and interpersonal bonds are strengthened.

17. Creating a Gratitude Trigger - Steps to re-wiring your mind to be focused on gratitude.

18. Becoming an empathetic citizen

As a trained clinical therapist and leadership coach, I feel compelled to offer simple talking points and healing tools for the leaders of a family to assist their tribe. While trauma can bring us to our lowest low, trauma also offers the opportunity of teaching how to listen and take good care of our own hearts and those around us. It is during times of crises that we are able to create a framework of life for our children to manage the challenges that they will have ahead. The openness, vulnerability and truth spoken during this time offers a necessary example to your children on how to take good care of their mind, body and spirit no matter what the current challenge.

Talking tool #1
It's OK not to be OK
When trauma happens, it is difficult for everyone and important to remember is that it's OK not be to be OK. Many times parents will share facts about what happens during trauma and avoid sharing emotions. Kids are intuitive and are able to sense the feelings of the people around them - especially their family. Just as you know when something is bothering your children, they know when something is bothering you.

As the family is going through challenges, it is important to tell the truth about what you are feeling even if it is not pretty, perfect or how you would like it to be.

Share with your children that we all have a range of emotions and when difficult things happen we all feel emotions like sadness, anger, irritation, frustration, etc. Check in with your children to see how they are feeling and role model with them how you are feeling. It is healthy for a child to understand that their parent is having difficult feelings about the situation and it is not about the child. For example, tell your child you are overwhelmed by all of the changes and tasks resulting from the hurricane and that you are not upset with the child. Let your child know it is normal to be sad and angry that your house got damaged in the hurricane and we cannot live there right now.

While a parent might think that saying "everything is ok" is good, hoping that their child will feel safe and fine, it actually does the opposite. Don't pretend it is all okay.

When parents lie to their children to give them a false sense of safety, that is exactly what they get… only a false sense of safety. When a human is lied to it erodes closeness and breeds distrust resulting in more feelings of anxiety and potential long term issues with trust.

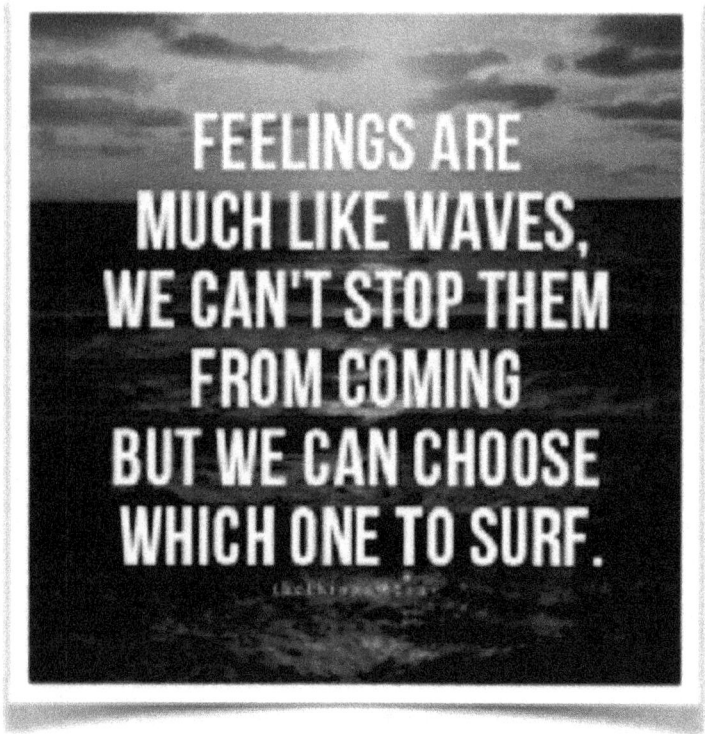

FEELINGS ARE
MUCH LIKE WAVES,
WE CAN'T STOP THEM
FROM COMING
BUT WE CAN CHOOSE
WHICH ONE TO SURF.

To help your children, let them know it is normal to go through many emotions when dealing with trauma. The top emotions with trauma are shock, fear, anxiety, anger, confusion, guilt, shame, sadness and feeling disconnected.

Role model a framework for talking about emotions. For example,
I feel _____ when the trauma happened.
The feeling of _____ is helpful for _____.
The feeling of _____ can be harmful when _____.
I have found that _____ helps me feel in balance and like myself again.

Example:
"I felt scared when the hurricane came. I know that anxiety is a
normal part of being human. My anxiety was helpful as it helped me
to be aware that we were unsafe and let me know we needed to
evacuate. If I don't manage my anxiety, it can be hurtful. I will get
easily irritated and will yell even over the littlest problem. Please don't
take my irritation personally. When my anxiety gets to be too much, I
have found that talking about it, exercising and/or doing breathing
exercises on youtube helps me lower my anxiety. What helps you?"
While this may seem like a simple exercise, it is a profound way to
teach your child how to name, accept and move through the difficult
emotions that happen in their life. Without guidance, many
individuals have not learned the shared human experience of how to
talk about and/or manage the difficult emotions we all feel and will
have more emotional difficulties in the future to manage. The
experience of learning why emotions are helpful and that they also
can be harmful empowers your child to increase their emotional
intelligence to be more successful personally and professionally in the
future. As your child recognizes when an emotion is beginning to
cause harm to self or others, understanding and being responsible for
ways to manage the difficult emotions will give your child self-esteem
and inner power.

Talking tool #2
How can difficult emotions be good?
Often times, people feel as if they should not have negative
emotions. Emotions are our internal indicators that teach us what is
right, good and true for our highest good. These talking points can
open up great conversation as to how your child is experiencing their
current emotions and those of the family. Remember, every person
has a unique experience on how they see, feel, hear and sense an
event. For example, you and your child both see an elephant. Your
child is standing in front of the elephant and loves its big floppy ears,
long trunk and kind eyes. You were standing behind the elephant
and have a much different perspective to share than your child.

When your child does share, be sure to honor and respect their feelings as they share. Be inquisitive, ask questions for clarity and thank them for sharing their unique and valuable experience that they are bringing to the world. If you find yourself wanting to correct or change the way they are feeling, take a moment to remember how important it is to have someone hear their heart without giving an opinion.

Below find some of the reasons that difficult emotions can be good to talk about with your children. **Shock** - Our mind and body will protect us when we hear news that is difficult or different from what we know or expect. When news is too overwhelming to manage, shock cushions the pain until we are able to integrate the new experience into our lives. Shock wears off little by little allowing the emotions that were too hard to bear surface as we are able to manage them. Be aware that after a trauma, it may take several months or more before shock will wear off. Ask your children:

Do you understand how shock can help us through trauma? What else do you need to understand?

Do you feel like they you still going through shock?

Do you feel like there is emotion deep down that has not got to come out yet?

Do you feel like anyone else in the family is going through shock?

Fear - Bravery and courage do not exist without fear present. One of the positive sides of fear is make us aware of our qualities of bravery, courage and ability to move through the difficult obstacles ahead of us. Once we have discovered our courage, we can use it over and over again to get out of our comfort zone into our next level of success. Fear also alerts us to dangers around us to help us get to safety.

Bravery and courage cannot exist without fear present - JnC

Anger - Anger is part of our survival skills. The feeling of anger arises when someone or something threatens us. We use anger to protect ourselves by running, fighting or finding a way to keep safe. Anger also alerts us that someone may have disrespected us, been unfair and/or caused us harm. It allows us to be aware that we may need to set better boundaries, seek clarity in communication or stop someone from hurting us.

Talking tool: What are other ways difficult emotions can be good? How do you know a negative emotion is beginning to hurt you and not serve you?

What can you do to manage your negative emotion?

Talking tool #3
Helping others in need

Many children have talked about feeling guilty that their family is okay when many others are struggling after a trauma. For example, "I am sad that my friend lost her home and I am worried about her". It is a normal human emotion to feel sad when my friend is hurt. It is good to have compassion when someone you love is hurt.

Talking tool

Brainstorm with your child what they would like to do to help?

- **Write a gratitude letter** to share with your friend how much they matter to you. Many children have related that because they may be displaced or struggling for basic needs, they feel worthless, ashamed and a burden. These feelings are not facts - they are just feelings and will pass as they are shared and as they see evidence that they are the same wonderful friend as they were before the hurricane. The great thing about gratitude letters is that it teaches your child the importance of gratitude for the wonderful friend that they have and sheds awareness for your child to continue a gratitude practice. The letter also gives light to where their friend's heart has been feeling dark.

- **Schedule a pizza/movie night** with the friend and/or the entire family. Allowing the child and/or family to step away from the stress and be a part of our one big human family can do tremendous good to lower stress and build community.
- **Start a fundraiser** - Bake cookies, wash cars, go through your toys and give one to a friend. Remember, what you feel like makes a small difference in the material world can make a profound positive change for the heart and healing of another.

Talking tool #4
Be aware of social media

Many parents grew up not having social media. Since social media began, children now have access to the view points of millions of others who can offer negative misperceptions about what is happening in the environment. The power of sharing the truth about what is happening externally and what is happening internally within the family mind and heart is imperative as it is guaranteed that people on social media will be sharing their emotions. It is important to understand that children can get caught up online and actually be re-traumatized online.

Talking tool:
Talk with the the family about a digital detox

Setting time limits around being online has been proven to reduce stress, allow people to focus more on true social interaction and connect with the healing aspects of available in nature.

After children have been online, be sure to ask open ended questions as to what positive and what difficult things they discovered. Keep in mind that kids could find out online that someone has been hurt, sick or died as a result of complications of the hurricane, lost their home, lost their pet, etc.

Talking tool: Ask open ended questions about what your child discovered online. For example, what are three things you discovered positive and negative online today? Be sure to listen without judgement to what they share. When children have a consistent experience that they can share the difficult things they found online without judgement, they will often initiate conversations about their concerns without you having to prompt. When your child shares something difficult, be sure to ask if they have any questions, want to talk more or just wanted someone to listen.

Talking tool #5
Get back to routine -
In the midst of all the changes, it is beneficial for children to get back into some semblance of a routine. Make it a priority in all the chaos to go back to helping with homework, having a scheduled dinner time, reading bedtime stories and whatever routine activities you had before the trauma. These basic activities can help lower the stress level in your child and give them something dependable to rely upon when there is so much change happening in their life due to the trauma.

Talking tool: What would help you most feel like you are getting back into routine? If your child speaks of ongoing anxiety, offer a plan from what you have learned to take precautions which help to lower anxiety.

Example: Create a safety code with your child that they can use at any time if they feel unsafe. For example, if your child is an unsafe situation, they can call and text you a safety code to let you know they need help. One family used a safety code of "I forgot to buy bananas" which meant I want you to come and pick me up because I am in an unsafe situation.

If your child is worried about hurricanes, share with them your step by step safety plan and ask if they have anything to add to the plan.

The word "listen" contains the same letters as the word "silent".

Talking tool #6
<u>Listening</u> -
When trauma happens, one of the most healing activities we can do
to help someone is to listen. Research shows that talk therapy works
because as you talk, listen to yourself, listen to the advice of others,
journal, read about the problem and try new things that you are
allowing more of your brain to work on the problem. When stress
occurs, we often run a problem through a standard set of solutions,
when the problem that we are having does not have a standard set of
solutions. We need others to help us to access more parts of our
brain and help us to brainstorm.
Often times, just having someone to talk about their experience is a
huge step in healing what they are experiencing. To be of service,
encourage yourself to become an experienced listener. Listening
means paying attention not only to the story, but the words being
used, the sound of the voice, how the other person "speaks" through
their body and your sense of the meaning. Listening involves hearing
a person's mind, heart, challenges and where they are on their path in
life's journey. Your ability to listen effectively depends on the degree
to which you perceive and understand all of the messages the person
is sending in both verbal and non-verbal messages.
It is important to note that being a good listener also offers an
environment of safety to speak current vulnerabilities. It is
recommended that the listener make it clear about their intentions to
offer confidentiality to the person that is opening up. After your
child has shared, be sure to repeat what you heard them say, validate
their feelings and ask what they need to feel safe now. Listening is
not a one time check in and is very valuable in the emotional health
of your child.
Talking point:
Create a safe space for open heart talks.
Share with your child that you would like to create a sacred place for
them to share their heart. In this space, you promise to listen to what
their heart has to say, where it is struggling and what it is learning
without judgement or punishment. This space is also a place where
what is said is held confidential, meaning that everyone agrees not to
share the conversation with anyone else. The only time that heart

talks will be shared outside the safe space is if there is a threat of safety that needs addressed. During heart talks, you also offer that you can listen without offering a solution unless it is requested. Explain to your child that sometimes we just need a safe outlet for our heart to speak. Other times, we might be seeking counsel from someone that has experienced the same feelings that we have and how to work through them. Offer your child the option that you are open to both just listen or offer counsel depending on what it is they desire. It is also very important to explain to children that they will not be punished for having difficult feelings. It is important to share that all humans have difficult feelings and it is during heart talks that they can share these feelings freely without getting into trouble. If your child shares a behavior that is causing them or someone else harm, it is important to clarify that this is a different matter of safety and will need to be addressed as a parent.

1) Pick a safe place to have heart talks. Where would your child feel most safe having talks about their innermost thoughts and feelings?

2) Discuss the ways that you will keep the safe space sacred: confidentiality, non-judgement, no punishment for sharing, and listening with or without guidance. Ask your child to share if there is anything they need in terms of confidentiality to open up. What are their fears about sharing? Will they practice asking for someone to listen if they are seeking counsel or needing to share?

3) Role model what your heart has to say, where your heart is struggling and what it is learning for your child.

For example, a mom recently shared with her daughter that she found out one of her friends was gossiping about her. The mom shared that her heart felt angry, betrayed and sad.

Her heart was angry and betrayed that someone she thought she could trust would speak ill of her to others. She feels sad as her heart does not want to remain friends with someone who would hurt her and she does not want to lose that friend. When she thinks about it, she feels as if she was stabbed in the back and a poison arrow pierced her heart. As such, she feels as if she has keep "watching her back" and needs to protect her heart around the woman who gossiped. She was struggling with whether or not to approach the woman about the gossip or to let it go.

When determining what she is learning, she recognizes her first priority is to protect her heart and do no harm to others. If she were to let it go and not share her feelings, she would have the options of releasing the role of friend from this woman to protect her heart or keeping this woman as a "friend" and possibly getting her heart hurt again. If she were to share her feelings that her heart was harmed by this woman's words, she would want to ensure that she spoke with clarity and grace as to do no harm to the other.

The mom can then thank her daughter for listening or may ask what her daughter felt was in the highest good for everyone.

The healing part about these conversations offers to children that they are not the only ones struggling and also gives a perspective for struggles that they might encounter in the future.

Talking point #7
Managing the stress monster

Stress can be healthy, beneficial and can even be life saving at certain times. It is when our stress levels get too high for too long that it can harm our mind, body and progress in life. When stress levels are too high for too long it is like a little angry monster sneaks inside you. It grows by feeding on the internal and external stressors in our life. It also loves to feed on drama, anger and fear and will seek situations in your life to get more fuel to feed on. The longer we allow the stress monster to grow within us, the more damaging the monster can become and the harder it can become to get rid of it. Until we are taught ways to deal with this monster, many of us will try to manage the stress by taking it out on ourselves making us tired, sad and even sending us into depression. Others will try and deal with the stress monsters by placing it outside of themselves. This means that they will often take it out on other people or things. These methods only distract you from lowering your stress and actually continue to feed the stress monster. The only way to get rid of the stress monster is to lower your stress in healthy ways. The stress monster does not like to leave and will fight to stay in your body. Just like monsters in the movies, the stress monster is deceitful and destructive as it lodges itself in your mind, your heart and your body. The next set of talking tools will provide you with exercises to help dislodge it from each of the places it lives within you. Some of these exercises will be things you have never tried before so please keep an open mind. Some may help immediately and others may take some time to see results. As you are a unique brilliant individual, certain exercises will work better for you than others and can lead you to finding even more tools to battle the stress monster. Remember that when you have defeated your stress monster you are able to think, feel, enjoy life and share who you are. As we all need you to share your unique gifts, the everyone in the entire world is rooting for you to beat your stress monster!

Talking tool: Children still have a very concrete mind. Having a tactile, tangible vision of the energy that is hurting allows more parts of the brain to have an understanding of the energy. Join your child in drawing a picture and name the stress monster. Be open that each and every family member may have a different vision and explain there is no right or wrong vision.

Talking tool #8
How the stress monster affects our body

It is really important that children know how stress affects the body so they can be aware of the signs and symptoms as their stress levels rise. As the stress monster gains power in our bodies, it can cause a variety of physical and psychological problems.

For example, since hurricane Irma, I've experienced "hurricane brain". Hurricane brain is what I call the effects of trauma on my thinking, affecting my short term memory and the feeling of brain fog. I will walk into a room with the intention of getting something and once I get there I have no idea why I came into that room. Be gentle with yourself and others as there is a biological reason for feeling like you've "lost" part of your mind. Research has proven that we are still wired to deal with stress as if we are cave people. The problem is that cave people coping skills were developed with the sole purpose to keep us alive. Since our minds and bodies have not been able to evolve with the pace of our technology and culture, we all still respond to stress with the same coping skills as we did 20,000 years ago. For example, a stressor for a cave person may be running into a bear and having to figure out a way to survive. In the modern world, our normal pressures now occur from school, friends, parents and social media that when left unattended can rise to levels that cause harm. Our bodies do not know how to judge what is raising our stress levels and will still respond as through we are being chased by a bear. This response to a high rate of stress is called the "fight, flight or freeze" response.

What is the fight, flight or freeze response?
The fight, flight or freeze response refers to physiological changes in the body) in response to stress.
What happens to the body?
- The heart speeds up
- Senses are dulled that are not currently needed
- Digestion slows down or stops
- Constriction of blood vessels in many parts of the body (Making your fingers and toes cold)
- Dilation of blood vessels for muscles (Your muscles ache)
- Pupils get bigger
- Tunnel vision (loss of peripheral vision - only able to focus on the current problem)

All of these changes in our body happen to keep us safe when we believe there is a stress that may cause us harm. What is interesting to think about is that our body can go into fight, flight or freeze from believing in an imaginary stress.

For example, have you ever watched a scary movie on television and felt fear flow through your body? For example, while watching a scary movie most people seem to develop super human hearing. When in fight, flight or freeze mode, even the smallest noise can startle us to believe that the scary monster on the movie is now somehow in our house. Another surefire sign that you are in fight, flight or freeze mode is you become so focused on the television that if someone comes up and touches your arm, there is a high probability that you will jump and react to that person.

Talking point: When have you felt fight, flight or freeze mode? Have you felt flight or flight:

During a scary movie?
When you heard there was a hurricane?
When you heard a loud noise at night?
When you saw a shooting on tv?
Are you replaying scary memories in your mind that are raising your stress thermometer? Would you be willing to rewrite the script?

Talking point #9:
Managing your stress thermometer:
Have you ever noticed that something little can unexpectedly send you into fight, flight or freeze mode and you don't know why?
For ease of understanding, think of your body as being wired with an internal stress thermometer that adjusts the body to relax or to move into fight/flight/freeze. To learn to monitor your stress thermometer, the first step is to figure out your healthy stress level. It is important to know that stress is not always a bad word. The human body needs a certain amount of good stress to function. For the purpose of your stress thermometer, think of a healthy level of stress thermometer functioning at about 30 degrees.
Under major stress (like running from a bear) your stress thermometer is wired to jump from 30 degrees all the way up to 100 degrees. As we discussed, at 100 degrees your mind and body unconsciously changes to ensure that you are able to survive the stressor by heightening the senses necessary (and dulling those not currently needed) to run or fight the stressor. In cave people times, we would lower our stress thermometers from running or fighting the bear. If I run from a bear, I will use up extra energy within my body to get away from the bear. When I get away from the bear, my brain registers that I am now safe and automatically takes my stress thermometer back to 30 degrees. The same applies if I were to stick around and fight the bear. If I fight off a bear, I will be using the excess stress created in my stress thermometer and if I fight off the bear, my stress thermometer returns back to 30 degrees.
As we head into the present, our stressors are made up more of time management problems, financial problems, relationship problems and other problems that are not easily solved by running or fighting them. The problem being is that our bodies have not caught up to handle lots of the little stressors that build up in our life. So these little stressors store in our stress thermometers and little by little we have so much stress stored inside it is like we are living at 95 degrees. When we go through trauma, we also store extra stress in our stress

thermometer that can make any little stress send us over the top. Trauma also affects our stress thermometer as there are often many minor traumas to deal with after the major trauma has happened. For example, evacuating for the hurricane or staying through the actual event of hurricane Irma caused all of us who went through it to have a stress thermometer at a hundred degrees. Once the hurricane passed, there were the new concerns of how my friends

Internal Stressors   External Stressors

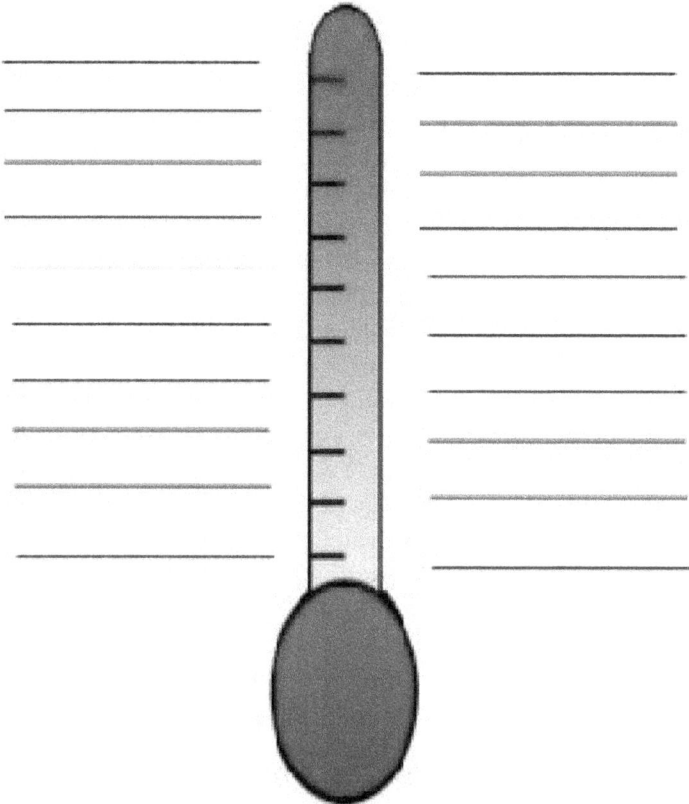

faired, how my home faired and when we could return to our beloved island. The concerns then changed to despair over those who lost t their homes, boats and lives. Helplessness and grief start to set in as your struggles are compounded by your whole community suffering. As clean up continues, there are other points of trauma and grief occurring as best friends, teachers and acquaintances move away.

Talking Point
What level is your stress thermometer currently at?
What is making your stress thermometer go up?
What makes your stress thermometer go down?
Activity: Join your child in drawing stress thermometers to place on the fridge so that everyone can learn to talk about where their current stress levels.
Throughout the day, move a magnet to show where your current stress levels are. It will not only strengthen personal awareness, but help to open conversations and compassion for what other family members are going through.

Talking Point#10
Activities for Moving Stress Out
Now that you have a visual for your levels of stress, it is important to learn how to let the stress move through you.
Whether you talk it out, write it out, cry it out, play, exercise... Just don't keep it in you!! If you do not find a way to release the stress, it will continue to build in your stress thermometer until you either you become physically ill, depressed or anxious. The most successful releases combine releasing the emotion both physically and mentally. We've already discussed a the powerful tool of talking it out and having a good listener to help you through trauma. Here are eight more ways to move stress out of the body.

1. **Write it out.** Writing an angry letter is a great release as you are able to release stress from both your mind and your body. When you are ready to write your angry letter, find a private space where you know you will not be interrupted. Write the meanest, nastiest, most viscous letter to the person or situation that is causing you the problem. Keep writing until you feel like you are done. When you are done, rip the angry letter up into little pieces. You can also stomp on it, yell at it or do anything that feels best for you before you throw it away. As you throw it away, be proud that you get rid of some the stress in your body.

2. **<u>Cry it out.</u>** Did you know that crying from emotional pain is actually one of your body's natural ways to relieve pain? When someone is crying from emotion, scientists have uncovered that different chemicals and hormones are released from the body than if you are crying from cutting up onions or it being windy. If you are overwhelmed and feel the need to cry, it is NOT a sign of weakness. It is actually your body asking you to release pent up pain. If you do not cry during the time that pain happened, you can release it later by triggering the emotion again. A trigger can be remembering the incident or even watching a sad movie.

3. **<u>Laugh it out.</u>** Laughter relieves stress, stimulates healing, exercises certain parts of the body, and helps in human bonding. Agree to find some laughter in your life every day. Challenge everyone in the family to find you a joke a day to share. There are so many ways to find laughter like watch a funny movie together, remember the funniest times of your life and relive them with someone, read a funny book, ect.

4. **<u>Exercise it out</u>** - Whatever exercise you prefer can decrease the production of stress hormones and counteract your body's natural stress response. When exercising, allow yourself the intention to "work out" whatever stress you had that day. You can even choose to mentally leave your stress at the gym and "work it out" again tomorrow. Whatever exercise you prefer does make a difference and agree with yourself that you going to ensure you continue exercising even during the most stressful times.

5. **<u>Sing it out</u>** - Music can connect us with the emotions of others. We have all heard songs that can make us feel excited, happy, sad, mad and many other emotions. When you are feeling stressed, allow yourself to find a song that you connect with and sing it at the top of your lungs. (I often do this while sitting in my car) Singing at the top of your lungs will help release the emotion and also expand your lungs to help with your breathing. Know that you are not alone in the emotions you are feeling can often be healing while releasing stored up tension that you have in your body. Once you have released the tension, play songs that make you feel happy and joyful to allow your body to fill with good vibrations.

6. **Draw it out.** As mentioned earlier, when you are stressed, the left side of your brain becomes dominant to where we often cut off the right side of our brain. Using creativity can open the bridge between your right and left brain. For this exercise, allow yourself to draw a picture of the person, situation or thoughts that are causing you stress. (An example of a drawing was a young lady who was hesitant to draw because she could not "think" of what her picture was to look like. I ask her not to "think" about it (as this was her left brain) and just "feel" what she thought it should look like. She ended up drawing a chaotic picture covering the page. When she stepped back and looked at what she had drawn, she realized that the picture represented how she was feeling as she felt her life had become chaotic.) Once you have the picture drawn out, you can take the next step to yell at it, jump on it, rip it up or whatever feels best to you to move the energy out of you.

7. **Be gentle...with yourself.** Often times when people get stressed, they yell at themselves. Please remember that everyone gets stressed and yelling at yourself for being stressed - will only stress you more! When you are stressed, learn to encourage yourself like you would a baby learning to walk. When a baby is learning to walk and stumbles and falls, you do not scream at the baby and say, "You are so stupid! All of the other babies learned to walk faster than you - you may as well quit!" Instead, you encourage the baby and inspire them to keep trying. Just as learning to walk was difficult at one point and has become second nature, so can your current goals. Be proud of yourself for getting back up and continuing to try when life gets tough.

8. **Seek Support**
One of the top tips in making progress is to ask for help. When problems arise, we often need different kinds of help. In general, there are three different kinds of helpers including good listeners, activity directors and pitchers. Although someone may be good at all of these activities, people are usually naturally good at just one of the ways to help others.

Talking Tool #11: What kind of helper are you?
As a therapist, I have seen many people get discouraged that others are not helping them in the way that they expected. I share with

people that as humans we are all wired differently with the way that we are good at naturally helping someone. To generalize, I share that there are good listeners, pitchers and activity directors.

Good listeners - These are the people able to sit and listen and actually hear what you have to say. They are not distracted and pay attention to everything that you have to say. They care about the problem you are currently facing. They are the non-judgmental friends and will not give you advice unless you ask for it.

Pitchers – These are the people that will pitch in and help with anything that you need. If you are sick, they will bring you chicken soup. If you break your leg, they will come over and help clean your house. They will do things to show you that they care.

Activity Directors – These are the people that will take you out to have some fun. They do not want to talk about the problems, they want you to take a break from it and enjoy life.

Talking tool:

Make a list of your friends and family. Determine which type of helper they are. Talk about how each of us has a different natural gift at helping and not to expect people to be good at all of them. Appreciate and love the person for how they are of service.

Talking point #12
Giving compassion

For those affected by trauma, we often have trouble hearing our heart after the event. Returning to my home in Key West after hurricane Irma passed, the suffering is palpable. Grief, stress and exhaustion is still easy to see in the eyes of our loved ones from having homes damaged, seeing the boats - the vessels that bring so much joy and abundance to many - wrecked and drowning and saying good-byes to the trees and flowers that have brought such beauty to our home.

In this space of vulnerability, each of us has the opportunity to offer healing to one another through kindness and compassion. Working as a therapist/coach for over twenty years, I've heard countless stories of how even the smallest act of kindness is able to help heal hearts that have been overwrought with trauma, pain, and grief... to allow the precious heart of another to remember the light when it has been lost in darkness. It is like a planting a seed of hope deep in the dirt. It might not seem like much at the time. It's still going to be dark in the dirt for awhile and the seed will have to crack open before it can push through the dirt to its new life. It feels like the same process to me for anyone who is going through trauma. Emotionally, it can get very dark. It can seem like you are cracking open and while you keep pushing, you haven't reached the surface yet leaving you feeling exhausted, depressed, anxious and overwhelmed. When an act of kindness enters that space, it gives the extra energy that we need to just sustain the current space we are in. Sometimes, an act of compassion can be the extra push to break through to the surface.

Talking point: Ask your child to think about:
The angry person you encounter today may have just lost their home.
The unreasonable person may have not had a good night's rest in at least a week.
The rude person may have countless loved ones in need right now and feel rushed to help.
Today, choose to be the kindness the heart next to you needs. It might be patience, it might be a smile, it might be a listening ear, it might be a hug, it might be letting someone go in front of you in line... there are a million ways to be kind... your heart will know just what to do.
We never know what the person next to us is going through or when we will be the one that is shoved back into the dirt to grow again. And that is just it... we will grow through this difficult space and bloom again... together.

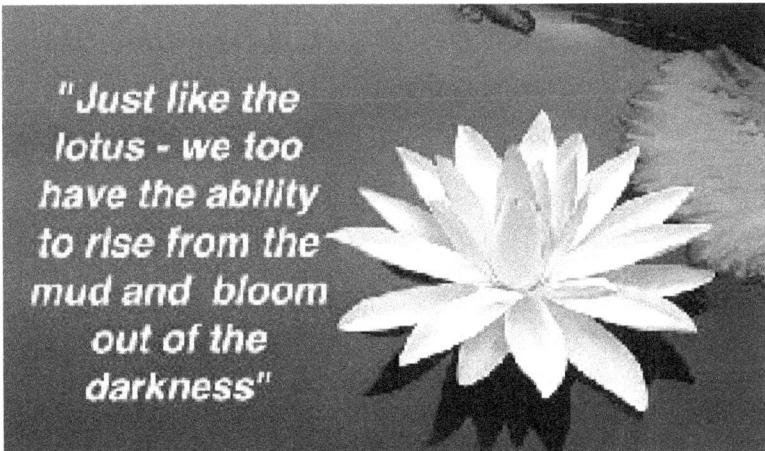

"Just like the lotus - we too have the ability to rise from the mud and bloom out of the darkness"

Talking tool
Compassion chats
Make time at the end of the day with your child to discuss what you did in compassion during the day. Did you offer a listening ear? Did you talk sweetly to yourself? Did you not take things personally? Often times, when I am struggling with compassion, I will remember that hurt people hurt people. If someone is causing me distress, I allow myself to picture that person free from suffering and remember the truth of who they really are. I am then able to realize how much they must be struggling in order to say or do something to cause so much pain to myself or others. I then ask myself what I can do to relieve their suffering. Sometimes, a person is not open to what I may have to offer and I remember that choosing to cause no more harm to that person in thought, word or deed is also a powerful way of giving compassion. As I offer this compassion to the other, I also offer it to myself that I can release what they did to harm me and free my heart to be safe, open, humble and shining again.

Talking point #13
Use Visualization
What is Visualization?
Visualization uses pictures in your mind to help change your emotions.
How can pictures in my mind change how I feel?
Research shows that your brain does not know the difference between actual or imagined events. So instead of watching a scary movie, you can train your brain to relax and access your right brain. When we visualize, we can create positive images for the mind that can then change our emotions and produce a more positive sensation.

You are already building new pathways. These thoughts lie down the foundation for pathways that you are going to be building. Top athletes, musicians, surgeons, business professionals and even the military have used visualization to be successful at their goals. Research confirms that visualization can boost athletic performance, especially with deep relaxation. One of the reasons is that as you begin to visualize, your muscles experience electrical impulses that correspond to the physical event you are imagining. In Golf My Way, Jack Nicklaus wrote: "I never hit a shot, not even in practice, without having a very sharp, in focus picture of it in my head. It's like a color movie." Another example is Liu Chi Kung. During the cultural revolution, he was imprisoned for seven years during which time he visualized playing the piano. When he was released, some say he played better than ever.

You allow yourself new possibilities! Visualizing a new goal allows you to try something new and prepare for what steps are ahead. It allows your brain to start thinking of new ideas, bring forth inspiration and looking for the resources necessary to meet your goal.

Important points to remember:

Visualize yourself doing your very best, with the absolute perfect form. If you are trying to improve your golf game and picture an incorrect form, you will continue to execute the incorrect form. Study where you need to grow and see yourself doing it.

Be specific. People often visualize general topics like "being healthy" or "making lots of money". Visualization works best if you "see" the specific steps and activities that will be needed to be healthy or make lots of money.

Practice often. Visualization works best if you "see" a little bit each day. If you try to cram a lot of visualization into one day, it will not be as effective as it is to visualize consistently over time.

Talking point #14
Visualization for tension

Take a moment to settle into a comfortable position.

Notice how you are feeling right now in this moment.

How does body feel? Scan your body and simply noticing how your body is feeling.

Scan the front of your body. Notice anywhere that you may feel tension. Scan the back of your body. Notice anywhere that you may feel tension. Place your hand over where you feel that tension. Now pull this tension out of your body and place it in your hands. Notice what this negative energy looks like, feels like, or sounds like. Take this negative energy and roll it into a ball. As you are rolling it, feel the negative energy of the ball turning into positive energy. Keep rolling and rolling until all of the negative energy has turned into positive energy. When this energy has turned into pure positive energy, allow the positive energy to flow back into the space you took the negative energy out of. Notice how the warm the positive energy feels as it flows in.

When you are ready, slowly open your eyes. Be grateful that you were able to transform negative energy into positive energy. If you need to, repeat this process again. Once you feel that you are full of positive energy, go and share your positive energy with others.

Talking point #15
Negative Thought Zapper Visualization

Take a moment to settle into a comfortable position. Close your eyes. Scan your brain for any negative thoughts that you are having. Picture these negative thoughts taking the form of an insect that has been flying around your brain "bugging" all of your other thoughts. Now picture that this bug flies out of your brain right into your hand. Peek into your hand and take a look at the bug. It has irritated you for a very long time and wants to go back in your brain. Tell the bug "NO!" I have a better plan for you. You look up and see a large bug zapper that transforms negative thoughts into positive thoughts. Tell your bug that you no longer wish to think this negative thought and throw the bug into the zapper. See your bug go into the zapper. As the thought that has been bugging you is zapped, it is transformed from a bug to a white light.

Ask this white light to enter your brain and fill it with peace and positive thoughts. Feel the white light entering your brain. Take a deep breath to allow all parts of your brain to be filled with this positive white light. Notice the warm feeling as the positive energy flows in.

You now can change your negative thought to a positive. Ask the light to give you a positive thought to replace the negative one. Just allow this thought to drop into your mind. When you are ready, slowly open your eyes. Be grateful that you were able to transform negative thoughts into positive thoughts. If you need to, repeat this process again. Once you feel that you are full of positive energy, go and share your positive energy with others.

Talking point #16
Create a gratitude ring

Every human being desires to feel safety, love, peace, happiness and connection. The Grateful Ring circle creates a way for people to share gratitude and create stronger interpersonal bonds.

In tribal wisdom, it is believed that when people feel loved, connected and grateful, they rarely commit harm against others. When a harm is committed, the tribe sees the behavior as a cry for help. As we all make mistakes, when someone does something hurtful and wrong, they take the person to the center of town and the entire tribe share the positive qualities and their gratitude for the person. The positive outpouring is to help reconnect the person to knowing that they are good, loved and accepted.

Steps to create a family gratitude ring

To learn the power of honoring one another's brilliance and sharing gratitude, one person from the family is placed in the center of a circle each day. Every member of the group shares with the selected person in the middle what they experience as this person's brilliance and why they are grateful for that person.

Each person states:

"I am grateful for you because..."

"I see your brilliance as..."

Each person of the group has an opportunity to sit in the middle of the circle.

It is recommended that each Grateful Ring is recorded by video/audio or transcribed so that the person will be able to connect back to it later.

Talking point #17:

Create a gratitude trigger

A trigger is an automatic, unconscious feeling paired with a external cue. When trauma occurs, our brain will store the smells, sounds, time, sights and other sensory data as a trigger to help keep us safe. For example, someone who has been shot at may feel the need to run when they hear fireworks. The brain also creates positive triggers. For example, you may feel relaxed and think of the beach when you smell coconuts. Science shows that with awareness and conscious effort, you can create your positive triggers to increase your immunity, boost positivity and help you to focus.

Research shows that we can create our own positive trigger by combining our thoughts and feelings with a visual/tactile reminder. For example, you may choose a wristband or purchase the I am grateful for... spinner ring specifically designed to create a positive trigger.

Science shows that the two most powerful times for your mind to be receptive is when you first wake up and right before you go to bed. In the morning, whatever you are thinking and feeling when you wake up is what your brain will look for the rest of the day to prove you right. If you wake up cranky, you will look for reasons to be cranky. If you wake up happy, your brain will look for reasons throughout the day for why you are you happy. It can be compared to the Google of your brain. If you don't change the search characteristics, it will keep searching for evidence of your last search. It is important to remember, that you have control over what your brain will look for throughout the day through conscious effort. Steps to a positive trigger:

1) Take the first ten minutes of your day to be in gratitude and combine it with your tactile/visual reminder. (Tactile/Visual - spinning your gratitude ring or changing your wristband from one wrist to the other as you think of reasons why you are grateful)

2) Wear a grateful ring throughout the day and whenever you notice something that you are grateful for spin your gratitude ring. Within about 30 days, your brain will pair spinning your ring with feelings of gratitude and automatically release gratitude each time you touch the ring. Since your feelings are faster than your thoughts, when you touch the ring, you will feel grateful and then your brain will look for reasons to prove you are right.

3) The last ten minutes of our day are also quite powerful. Whatever you are thinking/feeling before bed, you will spend the next several hours working on while you rest. If you are watching something that angers you before bed, your body will continue to process that anger while you sleep. Knowing that gratitude is one of the most healing chemicals for our bodies, take ten minutes before bed being in gratitude while also spinning the ring.30

4) As you practice building your trigger, you will find that touching the ring helps you become present to the moment and discover what is beautiful in that very moment.

Why choose gratitude to focus on?
Research shows that grateful thoughts increase immunity, decrease feelings of depression, decrease feelings of anxiety, improves sleep, fosters resilience and promotes empathy. Twenty seconds after thinking a grateful thought, your brain and body will be flooded with positive chemicals related to feeling grateful. The nervous system is then capable of reducing stress and pain in the body.
The more you think grateful thoughts, the more neurological pathways are formed that will help you feel better on a long term basis.

Talking tool #18

Empathetic Citizenship – A very powerful tool for moving through trauma is recognizing that we have the power to help others. After 30 days of building a positive trigger, ask your child to choose someone in the community to share their new knowledge about gratitude with and give the other person a gratitude ring. The process of sharing a gratitude ring has helped stop a teenager from committing suicide, connected people healing through cancer, reconnected relationships and many other powerful stories (read about them here).

Talking tool:

1. Have your child talk with you about the power of gratitude and the shifts they have seen in their life since starting this gratitude practice. Did they feel better? Did they notice more things that they enjoy in life? Did they sleep better? Did they notice that the positive trigger worked? Would they like to share this goodness with someone else?

2. Ask your child to think of someone that they are grateful to have in their life. Have them talk about and/or write down all the reasons they are grateful for the person. Once they have all the reasons complete, have your child practice speaking gratitude to another person. As you speaking gratitude, be sure to look the person in the eye and imagine your heart is speaking to their heart. Have them be specific as to why they are grateful for the person in front of them and then have them share all that they have learned through creating a gratitude trigger. Discuss with your child, that they can agree to be that person's gratitude buddy for one month and check in once a week to talk about what they are learning and how they are feeling with their new gratitude practice. This practice can build interpersonal relationship skills and compassion for others.

Join your child in sharing gratitude and becoming someone's gratitude buddy. You can choose to have one dinner a week sharing the power of how being a gratitude buddy can make a profound positive difference in someone's life and reinforce the actions of your child. Do a grateful ring:

Want to spread gratitude in your child's school?

Check out these free curriculums:

The short curriculum - Teaches practical tools to teaching gratitude for the self, for others and for the world in a classroom or in the workplace. This curriculum includes a facilitator guide, handouts and a powerpoint which is available on request.

The In-Depth Curriculum - Teaches the 9 steps to re-wire the brain, the science of gratitude and teaches practical tools to teaching gratitude for the self, for others and for the world. This curriculum includes a facilitator guide, handouts and a powerpoint which is available on request.

These are just a few of the powerful ways that can help the mind, body and heart after a trauma. Remember, you're doing a good job, you are loved more than you know and are showing up as a parent or you would not be reading this. The difference you are making by healing spreads farther and wider than you know!
Stay Blessed.

ABOUT THE AUTHOR

Jenny R. Craig, LCSW, BCD is a transformation coach known for her unique ability to help leaders and their teams look within and move past self sabotage. She offers practical and sustainable tools leading people to quantum leaps in personal and professional success. Passionate about teaching emotional intelligence, Jenny has spoken domestically, internationally and at the United Nations on tools for increasing emotional intelligence. As an innovator in brain-training tools, Jenny is the creator of the I am grateful for ring, numerous train-the-trainer programs, a six-week self-guided curriculum on emotional intelligence, author of four other books and has been part of two best sellers. Feel free to find out more at www.insitestrategist.com or www.gratefulring.com

www.ingramcontent.com/pod-product-compliance
Lightning Source LLC
Chambersburg PA
CBHW020954030426
42339CB00004B/97